MOON NEWS

Miller Williams Poetry Series
EDITED BY BILLY COLLINS

MOON NEWS

))) ○ (((

Craig Blais

The University of Arkansas Press
Fayetteville
2021

ISBN: 978-1-68226-161-3
eISBN: 978-1-61075-740-9

Manufactured in the United States of America

25 24 23 22 21   5 4 3 2 1

Designed by Liz Lester

♾ The paper used in this publication meets the minimum requirements of the American National Standard for Permanence of Paper for Printed Library Materials Z39.48-1984.

Library of Congress Cataloging-in-Publication Data

Names: Blais, Craig, author.
Title: Moon news / Craig Blais.
Description: Fayetteville: The University of Arkansas Press, 2021.
Series: Miller Williams poetry series | Summary: "Moon News, finalist for the 2021 Miller Williams Poetry Prize, deploys the sonnet form to treat subjects as diverse as Gregor Samsa, SpongeBob SquarePants, and the cosmos"—Provided by publisher.
Identifiers: LCCN 2020042351 (print) | LCCN 2020042352 (ebook) | ISBN 9781682261613 (paperback) | ISBN 9781610757409 (ebook)
Subjects: LCGFT: Poetry.
Classification: LCC PS3602.L337 M66 2021 (print) | LCC PS3602.L337 (ebook) | DDC 811/.6—dc23
LC record available at https://lccn.loc.gov/2020042351
LC ebook record available at https://lccn.loc.gov/2020042352

Funded in part by

MILLER AND LUCINDA WILLIAMS
POETRY FUND

238,900 miles and back,
give or take

CONTENTS

III ○ A Treasury of Saints & Martyrs

IV ○ Silver Millennium

SERIES EDITOR'S PREFACE

When the University of Arkansas Press invited me to be the editor of its annual publication prize named in honor of Miller Williams—the longtime director of the press and its poetry program—I was quick to accept. Since 1988, when he published my first full-length book, *The Apple That Astonished Paris*, I have felt keenly indebted to Miller. Among the improvements to the world made by Miller before his death in January 2015 at the age of eighty-four was his dedication to finding a place for new poets on the literary stage. In 1990, this commitment became official when the first Arkansas Poetry Prize was awarded. Fittingly, upon his retirement, the prize was renamed the Miller Williams Poetry Prize.

When Miller first spotted my poetry, I was forty-six years old with only two chapbooks to my name. Not a pretty sight. Miller was the one who carried me across that critical line, where the "unpublished poets" impatiently wait, and who made me, in one stroke, a "published poet." Funny, you never hear "unpublished novelist." I suppose if you were a novelist who remained unpublished you would stop writing novels. Not the case with many poets, including me.

Miller Williams was more than my first editor. Over the years, he and I became friends, but even more importantly, before I knew him, I knew his poems. His straightforward, sometimes folksy, sometimes witty, and always trenchant poems were to me models of how poems might sound and how they could *go*. He was one of the poets who showed me that humor had a legitimate place in poetry—that a poem could be humorous without being silly or merely comical. He also showed me that a plainspoken poem did not have to be imaginatively plain or short on surprises. He was one of my literary fathers.

Miller occupied a solid position on the American literary map, though considering his extensive career and steady poetic output, it's surprising that his poems don't enjoy even more prominence.

As his daughter became the well-known singer and recording artist that she is today, Miller came to be known as the father of Lucinda Williams. Miller and Lucinda even appeared on stage together several times, performing a father-daughter act of song and poetry. In 1997, Miller came to the nation's attention when Bill Clinton chose him to be the inaugural poet for his second inauguration. The poem he wrote for that event, "Of History and Hope," is a meditation on how "we have memorized America." In turning to the children of our country, he broadens a nursery rhyme question by asking "how does *our* garden grow?" Miller knew that occasional poems, especially for occasions of such importance, are notoriously difficult—some would say impossible—to write with success. But he rose to that occasion and produced a winner. His confident reading of the poem before the nation added cultural and emotional weight to the morning's ceremony and lifted Miller Williams to a new level of popularity and respect.

Miller was pleased by public recognition. What poet is immune? At home one evening, spotting a headline in a newspaper that read POET BURNS TO BE HONORED, Miller's wife, Jordan, remarked, "They sure have your number." Of course, the article was about an annual celebration honoring Robert Burns.

Miller's true legacy lies in his teaching and his career as a poet, which covered four decades. In that time, he produced over a dozen books of his own poetry and literary theory. His poetic voice tends to be soft-spoken but can be humorous or bitingly mordant. The poems sound like speech running to a meter. And they show a courteous, engaging awareness of the presence of a reader. Miller knew that the idea behind a good poem is to make the reader feel something, rather than to merely display the poet's emotional state, which has a habit of boiling down to one of the many forms of misery. Miller also possessed the authority of experience to produce poems that were just plain wise.

With Miller's sensibility in mind, I set out to judge the first year's contest. I was on the lookout for poems that resembled Miller's. But the more I read, the more I realized that applying such narrow criteria would be selling Miller short and would not be fair to the entrants. It would make more sense to select manuscripts that Miller would enjoy reading for their own merits, not for their similarity to his own poems. That his tastes in poetry were broader than the territory of his own verse can be seen in the variety of the books he published. The list included poets as different from one another as John Ciardi and Jimmy Carter. Broadening my own field of judgment brought happy results, and I'm confident that Miller would enthusiastically approve of this year's selections—winner Michael McGriff's *Eternal Sentences*, finalist Craig Blais's *Moon News*, and finalist Madeleine Wattenberg's *I/O*—as well as those of previous years.

o

If I had to give a Hollywood elevator pitch on behalf of Michael McGriff's *Eternal Sentences*, the 2021 Miller Williams Poetry Prize winner, I might say that it's a blend of the low-rent sociology of Raymond Carver with the quirky imagination of Richard Brautigan. The speaker of these poems lives in the realm of Kmart, McDonald's, and Gas Qwik. Friends are in jail. A snake is coiled inside a Schlitz can, the family is too proud to accept food stamps, and the neighbors are "too poor for a fence." But that, compared to the method and power of these poems, is just the scene, not the subject.

The title of this book is very explicit about what lies inside, that is, a series of sentences. Of course, we could describe just about all writing from the Bible to Jim Thompson as a progression of sentences, but here the sentence is king. I was enjoying myself so much on first reading that I failed to notice right away the distinguishing scheme at work in every poem. Each line of every poem is its own periodic sentence, where the reader must fully stop before he or she can go on. And the period is the only punctuation allowed in this collection, apart from a handful of apostrophes just to keep track of who owns what. The comma, a useful way to guide the sentence and control its rhythm, is banned. The period rules. The deeper we wade into McGriff's collection, the more we realize that while the exclusive use of end-stopped sentences, one after the other, is the source of the poems' power, it is also a self-imposed restriction. It reminded me of W. S. Merwin's comment that he abandoned (or transcended!) punctuation in order to make writing poems more difficult for himself by doing without its help. Here, every one of McGriff's poems is a box of sentences.

Such a repetition of short, declarative sentences risks the monotony some associate with the lockstep heroic couplets of eighteenth-century English poetry. But the sentences here, for the most part, are a wonder. Whether linked to create a suggestion of a narrative or, just as commonly, to not strain toward a singular point, the stacks of sentences are always fresh and often striking. Some are straightforward:

> "I wore the same jacket to your wedding and your funeral."
> "My sandwich tastes worse than I thought."
> "They're poking at a fire with curtain rods."

Others are quirky, surrealistic:

> "A skyful of sparrows poured from my chest."
> "I try to step through a mirror discarded in an alley."
> "Three early stars torqued into place along the border."

And the hand of Brautigan is present:

> "The elk sharpen their craft of disregarding us."
> "Everyone from the eighteenth century looks seventy-five and doomed."

Eternal Sentences makes us reexamine the line in poetry and the sentences that lines can hold. Charles Olsen ordered that "no line must sleep." The lines gathered here could not be more aroused, aware, and wakeful. Here's one poem in its entirety:

Tonight I Am

A dead flashlight in a kitchen drawer.
A sheet of three-cent stamps.
A fistful of gravel as a last defense.
Wind against the house lying through its teeth.

This series of short sentences produces both individual eye-openers as well as some overlap that suggests possible patterns.

One leaves these poems with the feeling that life comes at us in a series of sentences too stark to be interrupted by the brake-tapping of a comma. I've heard metaphors for life that hold less truth. *Eternal Sentences* will come at its readers as a series of happily endless delights.

o

To return to the elevator for a moment—*Moon News*, finalist for the 2021 Miller Williams Poetry Prize, can be seen as the unlikely marriage of Charles Bukowski and Sir Philip Sidney, but of course, that doesn't do justice to Craig Blais, who is a strong and engaging poet in his own right. We can say that *Moon News* is a collection of sonnets if we allow that a poem cast in the basic shape of a sonnet is a sonnet. The shadow of the English sonnet is visible here: fourteen lines divided into three quatrains and the couplet. But the quatrains are not grammatical units as they tend to be with the Elizabethans; rather, they run on into the next quatrain and finally into the couplet, amen. This is the more urgent, jumpy sonnet in which the poet talks through the shape of the poem, hurrying ahead until he feels the couplet nearing; then he finds a way to use the two remaining lines to close the poem up. As readers, we experience both the familiarity of the sonnet box and the many novel twists and odd surprises of this poet's original hand. In one poem, Blais's grandmother's pea soup recipe acts as the closing couplet. In other scenarios, the couplets sound like items from a police blotter or a nurse's log. This is the sonnet repurposed for our time.

Here's one example from a stack of endings. The speaker is sitting at home watching a football game and drinking "a thirty-pack" when a friend stops by and declares he is "interested in exploring 'traditional / masculine gender roles.'" And here are the lines that directly follow:

The sun is reversing

its magnetic field every eleven years—flipping
end over end like a chariot tossed by horses

off the road and down a rocky embankment.
North becomes south and south north as it follows

an orbit around a galaxy center that flails its arms
like a wide receiver looking for a penalty flag.

That is not allowed in prose, and it shows Blais's full awareness of the high degree of imaginative freedom offered by poetry. To read these poems is to be both enclosed by the sonnet's chalk lines and released by the wildness of the content. The swerves of thought are not dictated by the sonnet's divisions. A poem that begins about a friend schooling the poet for his drinking ends this way: "Molten iron / converts to steel and hardens until the next thing // you know, there are 446 bridges in your city / and a weapon for every imaginable atrocity." Poems, it has been said, should at least be interesting—and these are in spades. Speaking of which, a woman reading tarot cards is "bluffing like she's in the middle of a poker game." The poet writes someone's phone number on a rock and tosses it into his backyard in case he ever locks himself out of his house; he does this because "I am scared."

Most poets in America teach. Blais is in the minority who admit the experience into their poems. In teaching Kafka's *Metamorphosis*, he deals with one student who says, "'That's weird.' / The same thing he's said all semester about everything." Another thinks Gregor—the "bug-man"—"brought it on himself somehow." Or "his family did it to him." Finally, the "weird" kid is given the couplet: "'Maybe it's not about *why*. Maybe it's about / how everybody left behind just has to deal with it.'" In another poem about teaching English, the students are unimpressed when told "that *stanza* in Italian / means *room*," so teacher tells them it really means *crime scene*.

Moon News modulates into a series of sonnets about Saint Blaise, "patron saint of animals and those suffering from throat ailments." Here reverential prayers mix with hagiographic exaggerations: "Like Jesus, Blaise walked on water, but unlike Jesus, / when he got to the center of the lake, he sat down." Another section is a kind of elegy for friend "Alex," but the tone is mixed like the tone of this whole book. The sonnet never before carried such cargo: heroin, hospital rooms, poems growing out of trees and out of a person's open hand, a flower drooping "like it could give a fuck," Jeff Bezos, Tom Brady, and SpongeBob himself.

Moon News is a dazzling collection of fully American sonnets. And if you want to get the real moon news, Blais will tell you that "the moon appeared after earth took a glancing blow / off the chin 4.5 billion years ago. // Every day since it has been tugging at our seas / like a child afraid its mother will leave."

○

Io, you might recall, was one of the lovers of Zeus who was turned into a heifer then back into a woman. And in *I/O*, she holds a lantern to guide a poet through a book of poems, for Madeleine Wattenberg is a votary of this goddess. Io is her confidante and confessor. It is Io to whom her letters are addressed, as if the poet had one foot in the ancient world of mythology and the other in her own time. In opening up a channel between her personal history and the age of mythology, the poet develops a private association with Io and her time. *I/O* is peppered with questions as if the poet sought answers to her own unfolding journey: "Io, tell me how you left the grove." "Tell me how you crossed the sea with only a gnat for company." "Were you surprised when Hera took you into the grove and fastened your gold collar?" The poems seem to toggle back and forth between ancient and modern realms, with the ancient world dominating the sensibility and the sound of each utterance. Even when the poet is in her own time, her language sounds vaguely elemental, as if she wants to be better understood by Io. Subtle, intentional missteps in grammar and diction signal an effort to write in a more basic English with a more ancient sound. Nature is even animated as it would be in a mythological world: "The hills shift their shadows as though swinging a load from hip to hip." Her more natural language is tinged with a delicate sensuousness. She is "careful not to tear the purple skin" of a plum. She announces that "I don't wash my hair for ten straight years / and each day the oil drips down my back."

And while swimming, "Underwater, my feet / glitter like pink cities." And many of Wattenberg's poems sparkle with stunningly inventive images, as when trees spread "like tails of peacocks to the sky" or "the clouds remain closed as caskets."

Another female figure enters the scene with Margaret Cavendish, the seventeenth-century poet, scientist, and pioneer feminist who published under her own name and challenged the belief in a mechanistic world. We get a view of the duchess's complex laboratory. Cavendish appears in a poem titled "Uses for Late Frost," which recalls a scene from her groundbreaking novel *The Blazing World* in which "a merchant abducts / a daughter as she gathers / shells along the shore." The lines that follow—"They sail to where two / worlds meet"—reminded me of how Wattenberg makes the two worlds of today and ancient Greece meet through the agency of Io.

For me, the poem that best represents the strange power and imaginative pressure of this book is "Charon's Obol," in reference to the coin that those being transported to the underworld must give the ferryman. The myth serves as background and grounding wire to the poet's growing up, from her father placing on her tongue "a sliver of peach / or a white pastille . . . a homeopathic moon," to her tongue "sliding against the edges of men," including "a boy who tastes of copper." Finally, the coin becomes the obol of death. The poet practices dying by placing "a coin / across my tongue." "How can I know which boat to board," she asks in terminal confusion, "I'm just trying to pay my way." *I/O*, despite its brief title, is a book of expansive power and enviable craft.

Congratulations to all three of these poets. The University of Arkansas Press is honored to be the home for these titles for years to come.

Billy Collins

ACKNOWLEDGMENTS

Thank you to Billy Collins, David Scott Cunningham, Janet Foxman, the Miller and Lucinda Williams Poetry Fund, and everyone at the University of Arkansas Press.

Thank you, too, to the editors at the following publications who supported and encouraged this work by publishing individual poems herein: *Anti-*, the *Antioch Review, Barrow Street, Cimarron Review, Denver Quarterly, Hotel Amerika, Huesoloco, Lake Effect*, the *Los Angeles Review, The Moth, New Orleans Review, New Welsh Review, Prism*, the *Southern Review, Sugar House Review, Western Humanities Review*, and the *Yale Review*.

I ∘ In the Pines, in the Pines

NE 38 – BUF 30

Someone suggested I try to write a sonnet
about a night I'll never remember. "It doesn't
have to be *real*," I was told, like I'm unaware
that every poem is at least part fiction.

I nail the undeniables like rusty stakes
through the fog: Just one game—two or three pops.
The tiki-style bar whose name I can't remember.
Aaron Hernandez with six receptions and one drop.

Ten hours later: A wet receipt plastered
to the varnished bar top. I drive home a 9
out of 15 on the Glasgow Coma Scale. The face
of the kid dragged the last mile under my car

looks up at me like a stranger with eyes I know
come clawing through the night to rescue me.

Moonflower

And I wrote this one because every poet (especially
a sonneteer like myself) needs at least one poem
about flowers, so when that one guy asks
when drinking beers in the hockey rink parking lot,

"Hey, I heard someone say you were a *poet*.
What the fuck do you write about?" you can move
the conversation along as quickly as possible
with the stock answer: "Flowers mostly,"

and everyone can get back to trying to impress
the one girlfriend who made the mistake of coming
out that night to watch your meaningless game.
"How's this for a flower?" a winger shouts, as the moon

illuminates the curling petals of his two DUIs
and one pink slip he raises over his head for all to see.

I Hate Myself and Want to Die

1.

I never cared much about dream analysis until
I started losing limbs and spitting out teeth
then lost the whole bottom half of my body
and floated down empty hospital halls like a ghost.

That was twelve years ago. All the books said I said
something I regretted. This morning I drink coffee
from a hand-me-down mug behind my house, turning
in circles as bumblebees fight or fuck midair

like tiny chainsaws. When their bodies clash the discord
amplifies like the sound of static between stations
on the radio dial. After this, I put my laundry
in three plastic grocery bags, grab my sunglasses,

and drive down Florida's Space Coast, tailgated
by one nagging thought I can't seem to shake.

2.

After twenty years, I'm listening to Nirvana again,
even the polished overdubbed singles
that are so burned into my memory the recordings
seem redundant. It can take a long silence

to finally hear something anew, like a noisy
and lurching deep cut left off their last record,

which Kurt Cobain himself dismissed by saying,
"I can write that kind of song in my sleep,"

and so sold it for sixty thousand dollars
to *The Beavis and Butt-Head Experience* album.
Thrashing and nonsensical, the song was given
a title Cobain had to have known he would be

asked to explain. It was meant as a joke, he told
Rolling Stone, "as literal as a joke. Nothing more."

3.

My mother and grandmother have been eating
vegan for four months, so we have yellow pea soup
cooked without salt pork, even though it's eighty
degrees outside, then I pet the cat and put my feet

in the pool while my laundry dries. There are Bud Lights
behind the leftovers in the bottom of the fridge.
My grandmother's arms are covered in dark purple
bruises and her hair is no longer permed. She wears

a headband like an elementary schoolgirl
to keep her bangs out of her eyes and watches
the television Westerns we always thought were
on for my grandfather. She is sunken deep

into the overstuffed recliner and we exchange
a clumsy half-hug the last time we say goodbye.

4.

All this driving up and down Route 1 might explain
why I dream these days not of amputation
but of swimming in a gray ocean—not away from
or toward the shore, but a hundred yards parallel to it.

The dream dictionaries say it means I'm showing
great courage, not drowning, no matter how often
I fill the pockets of my swim trunks with those
sister stones: *I hate myself* and *I want to die.*

"They're called automatic thoughts," my therapist
says, "Empty phrases you got in the habit
of repeating until they gained privilege over
countless alternatives, like *Oh well, whatever* . . ."

"Nevermind," I want to say—but avert my eyes
like she has the power somehow to read my mind.

5.

It was how Kurt liked to answer those who asked
how he was doing: "I hate myself and want to die."
He told a reporter, "I thought it was a funny title."
Across the bridge of the song, a spoken bit lifted

from a recent episode of SNL: MOST PEOPLE
DON'T REALIZE THAT LARGE PIECES OF CORAL, WHICH HAVE
BEEN PAINTED BROWN AND ATTACHED TO THE SKULL BY COMMON
WOOD SCREWS, CAN MAKE A CHILD LOOK LIKE A DEER.

It is the same as saying it doesn't matter;
this space can be filled by literally anything.
"We knew people wouldn't get it; they'd take it too
seriously. It was satirical, just making fun of ourselves."

A B-side to "Pennyroyal Tea," the song was released
then recalled a month later, after Kurt killed himself.

6.

When I arrive home, I remember a night when
I was nine, my mom and dad fighting a year
before he died, him calling me as he stormed out
to go collecting for the family paper route.

After I gathered a few bucks, and after
he updated his little blue notebook under
the dim light of the station wagon, we circled
back home: "Stick with me, kid. We'll go places."

He said it so casually I thought he made it up.
What did I know about film noir archetypes—

of parody, sarcasm, or situational irony?
I thought one day I'd hear him call my name again

and we'd be gone, far from our streets, into the gulf
of darkness where words and reality meet.

Wait for It (a Sonnet with Language off a Coffee Mug)

BIRDS OF A FEATHER FLOCK TOGETHER . . .
my mother's coffee mug reads in squiggly letters
beside two pink flamingos in dark sunglasses.
She clouds the Folgers Classic Roast

with creamer until they whirl into one inside
the cup (no sugar) before lifting it to her lips
each morning after coming home from the nightshift
on the Sweet Life loading docks. This isn't the time

for her to hear my needy teenage pleading
for a signature or five bucks. Sip after sip,
I watch out of the corner of my eye as it rises
a little higher each time until, finally,

I can see the punchline hidden on the bottom
of her half-empty cup: WANNA FLOCK?

Sonnet (with Language from Clothes Crumpled on My Floor)

When I ask if she feels as empty as me
after, she tells me her whole life story: white sand
and neglect. I learn more from reading the waistband
of her G-string panties—RAMPAGE INTIMACIES

MADE IN MACAU—as I pick them up before the cat
gets at them. She wants me to ball them up and shove
them in her mouth, a makeshift muzzle
with a strip of duct tape. But I want a salad.

I've lived in as many places as her clothes have
manufacturers—HONDURAS, Wichita, CHINA,
San Francisco, LESOTHO, Seoul, DOWNTOWN LA,
North Florida—and I'm sure this isn't the last

place I'll seek the "geographical cure." 99%
one thing, a tag reads. And 1% something else.

Sonnet (with Language Etched into the Corner of a Bus Window)

A hawk circles above the tobacco barn as
off-duty firefighters help assemble a
merry-go-round. Hungover and smelling of
wood smoke on Sunday morning. PPC-25C AS

-4 superimposed over a maize maze
farmers have flattened into the face of Jesus,
"Man of the Year." I still don't know how to treat
anyone in my life. When I close my eyes, I see exes

with ELECTRIPLEX® and FRA TYPE I TIER II
tattooed on their lower backs. Every part ordered,
"bearing the owner's name someway in the corners,
that we may see and remark, and say *Whose*?"

The barricade surrounding the mechanical bull
was made from the fused frames of old bicycles.

Speed Demons

1.

That's what my dad called the fast kids on offense
sent on streak routes when playing touch football
in the street in front of the house. He was the devil
himself, but near the end we were lucky to see one sprint

a game before he returned to the protected
pocket of automatic quarterback. That's the speed
the child wants to see: the wily guy fleeing—
even though evolutionary biologists say

we run not as a result of being hunted
but because we were hunters who moved in small packs
on the Serengeti. Not the fastest animal
but the most persistent, trailing larger mammals

for tens of miles, isolating the weak ones,
and forcing them to collapse under a blazing sun.

2.

When things went on for too long, one might stop
while the others continued, and when the lagging
hunter caught up, another would drop back,
careful not to lose sight of the fading pack.

When he was dying in Boston, my brothers and I
watched the Olympics. Ben Johnson broke

the hundred-meter world record in Seoul
and two days later had his medal taken away.

I like to think that if my dad had survived another
recovery awaited him, one that would have stopped
his running himself down like a natural enemy.
The evening news kept showing Johnson frozen

on the starting blocks. Crouched down in a cloud of dust.
Sometimes any movement at all is too much.

Nuisance Animals

1.

"You know the money doesn't go to bears,"
Kay says as we sit at a traffic light behind
a beige Prius with charity plates of a black bear
standing on its hind legs while in the background

a white egret takes flight. "It goes to sea turtles."
She would know—environmentalist and Florida native.
There is a database for each type of plate,
tracking year by year how the money is spent.

Kay knows databases too. At her job
she takes calls and updates a satellite map
of bear sightings across the state, marking coordinates
with a digital flag pin and brief description:

LARGE ADULT SPOTTED HEADING NORTHWEST AT DAWN.
DISAPPEARED INTO THE PINES OF THE SIDE YARD.

2.

Most callers are friendly. Most welcome her advice
that they scrub their grill tops, keep fruit from the compost,
and remove any birdfeeders from their back deck.
Most of those in towns along the wildlife corridor

jump at the excuse to share their tale of a chance
encounter with a three-hundred-pounder at dawn

as it rummaged through the garbage on the curb.
Trash is the number one culprit. Lock-top cans the answer.

Some men though can't accept that the solution
is that they do nothing. They say if it keeps up
they will have to take matters into their own hands.
They're done playing by the rules. Some tell Kay

they like the sound of her voice, and they want to know
if she'll come out to investigate the matter personally.

3.

There are agents who deal with nuisance bears.
"Licensed Wildlife Rehabilitators," to be exact.
No longer officially threatened, they are still
protected under Bear Rule: 68A-4.009,

which states that a bear can only be "taken" when
"no non-lethal options can provide practical
resolution . . ." Kay's office is littered with tools
of the trade—artifacts that are recycled as teaching

materials at county fairs: twelve-gauge beanbags,
bright yellow paintballs, and punctured sardine cans
taken out of traps like readymade art. The most
popular item though is the bowl of teeth. Children

sift through it to find the sharpest points, pressing them
into their fingertips to test the strength of their skin.

For Kristofer V.

1.

I was six states away and halfway through my morning
ritual when I heard the news. A weeklong heatwave
in Wichita. 105 degrees at 6 p.m.
It all clicked into place so quickly some part of me

thought I already knew. That's what's changed the most
in the last eight months: I allow myself thoughts like
maybe I already knew. Every morning I read
out back, turning my chair to follow the sun

until it disappears over the roof. My spirit
animal is the heliotrope as I shift
one inch to the right . . . to the right . . . The pineal
gland is stimulated by bioelectrical input

received through the eyes, making me feel something
like happiness. But I've been calling it gratitude.

2.

Flashback to a Sunday afternoon in the house
on Fairmount Ave.: I was drinking a thirty-pack
and watching the Patriots. Tinfoil-extended
antenna bending off the ceiling. Pakistanis

playing cricket in the street out front, and you
stopped by with a friend for free beer but said you were

interested in exploring "traditional
masculine gender roles." The sun is reversing

its magnetic field every eleven years—flipping
end over end like a chariot tossed by horses
off the road and down a rocky embankment.
North becomes south and south north as it follows

an orbit around a galaxy center that flails its arms
like a wide receiver looking for a penalty flag.

3.

The sun is mine. Soundwaves tunnel through it
to form electrical patterns that mirror my own.
I believe my own consciousness is the byproduct
of bioelectrical patterns received from the sun.

You believe it's a brute ball of unconscious gas
burning in a vacuum. Everyone has to
believe something. René Descartes thought
the pineal gland was the seat of the soul

and that it fills with sand when neglected. My soul,
like the sun, oscillates. It swings in the breeze like
an open-mouthed mask hanging in a vineyard
the size of a grain of wheat. It casts shade

small and empty as a grave. I miss you, Kris,
and I wish I had the right words to say.

4.

Before you left, I went in the other room and grabbed
a City Lights book, *Poetry and Mysticism*.
Among other things it breaks down a symbolic
system dreamt up by W. B. Yeats so complex

the author doubts Yeats himself believed in it.
But it kept him working. You looked at it casually
and flipped it to your friend, "He's the one who's into poetry."
What could I have said? *To make it long in this world*

you need to love something? To love something,
you need to see you and it as one? Better to have said,
Why should all these dumb fucks live and not you?
We are supposed to let something lie to us

until we are shaking with its energy. (The sun,
Kris, the sun.) We are all still here burning up.

II ∘ Songs from the Rooms

1. A Sonnet Made of Steel

John tells me what he remembers about my drinking
is how I didn't take breaks in between to let
the body "process" them. I quietly resent
the way he's the expert now because he didn't

quit. I resent how I now use words like *resentment*.
But John is the expert after having spent
months of his life across the table from me
as I tossed back one after another while we

took turns reading Joyce or Carver or Maupassant.
My first thought is to do something with this info,
but some wisdom comes too late. Molten iron
converts to steel and hardens until the next thing

you know, there are 446 bridges in your city
and a weapon for every imaginable atrocity.

2. For Jim W. (Woodville Hwy, Tallahassee, Fla., December 9)

On my way to the memorial service for
a friend I never met who ended it all Monday—
A $9.99 RIB EYE! sign and two guys burning
a pile of leaves when a gray bird bounces softly

off the right corner of my windshield and I watch
in the rearview to see if it flies up to the
canopy of branches above or drops to the
road below, but I see nothing and point my eyes

forward again—ROCKS FOR SALE • BACKHOE FOR RENT—
a group of six double-wides with a hand-painted
sign: BUDDYVILLE. Nobody fucking knew a thing.
That's the gist. I leave early blaming the Saint Francis Prayer.

O DIVINE MASTER, GRANT THAT I MAY NOT SO MUCH SEEK TO BE
CONSOLED, AS TO CONSOLE; TO BE UNDERSTOOD, AS TO
UNDERSTAND; TO BE LOVED, AS TO LOVE . . .

Windows down, sun out. Centennial Bank blinking
76° / 3:15 p.m. / 76° / 3:15 p.m. / 76° / 3:15 p.m.

3. Safehouse Sonnet

This isn't the first time I've been run out
of town, but it's the first time I've flipped the couch
on its side and pushed it in front of the window
with you. The first time we've taken the legs off

the kitchen table to block the sliding glass door.
Though we both know safety isn't measured
in the strength of a hideout's defenses but in
its seclusion, I jam a chair under the doorknob

like they do in black-and-white gangster movies
when a dame as comely as you sits on the bed
and a guy as high-strung as me paces the wood floors
waiting for the worst to happen. We wait as if

for a hail of bullets, nondescript knocking, or
a Molotov cocktail to fuse our fates in fire.

4. Birthday Night Sonnet

How much are any of us indebted to those
we hurt? And what can they give that will make up for
I KNOW WHAT WD-40 TASTES LIKE CUZ I'VE HAD A GUN IN
    MY MOUTH
the pain they caused? We are so alone in our hurt.

And why not? "There is no need to explain or com-
pare," William Carlos Williams wrote, "Make it and it
is a poem." We might kill or beat to a pulp
someone on the fringes so the one who caused

us pain can look at the devastation and feel
the same mix of senseless disgust and betrayal.
MY ADDICTION IS OUT IN THE PARKING LOT DOING PUSH-UPS.
This is how we seek justice and share our hate.

This is how we turn the whole world on ourselves.
And think, DON'T BELIEVE EVERYTHING YOU THINK.

5. Death Card Sonnet (Cassadaga, Fla., Black Friday)

The image appears to be of a bishop holding
an infant up to armor-clad Death on its white steed,
as if to say, *Take this thing. Not me.* Though, really,
the baby's only a shadow cast by the setting sun.

When she places the last card, Reverend Candi's
bluffing like she's in the middle of a poker game,
not at the end of a tarot deck: "You have to be
careful the past doesn't pull you down," she states.

"Wait, wait, wait, wait . . . It doesn't mean I'm gonna die?"
"We're all going to die," she answers predictably.
"This is just a bad chapter. By June or July
you should turn the page." Next, she'll tell me

the king splayed out on the ground is just sleeping
and the horse's eyes burn red because the sun is rising.

6. Oh Lovely Rock (a Sonnet with a Phone Number in It)

I wrote your number on a rock and tossed it in my
backyard; should I ever lock myself out with no
phone, I'd be able to comb through the hollow
stemmed crabgrass where the cat used to piss when I

still let her outside (before she hopped the fence), and
then I could knock on my neighbor's door, borrow
her cell, and call 682-4840
to ask you to come over, please, with my spare key.

That's the kind of shit I dream up all the time
because I am scared. Because I am scared I
made this rock—its slow-moving atoms capable
of bearing the weight of a mountain—wear my scrip

like an *A* it shrugged off after a year, as if
to say, *Nothing can save you, kid. Stop trying.*

7. Sonnet (as an Excuse to Publish a Story Written when I was Ten)[1]

WHAT A WORLD crossed out and replaced by
WHY ME. I see the dilemma: decades later
I am still unsure which is better.
What I think I was trying to get at wasn't why

JUST NOTHEN SEEMS TO GO RIGHT so much as
why Mrs. Chiconis (and the rest of the class?)
should feel sorry for me. But glaring—
after the litany of personal injuries and

misspellings—is what's missing, a fact I'm too
willing to share as an adult, and which makes me miss
the kid who didn't put it out there, the one who'd
search his whole body over for scars and phys-

ical trauma a thousand times instead
of uttering four simple words: *My dad is dead.*[2]

---

1. As a footnote.
2. "Why Me"
Hi I'm Christafor Stallwell sometimes I think I have the worst life. In this
Univirse. Mabey not the worst but one of the worst. It's just nothen seems to
go right. I think it started the day I was born. It all started June 11, 1978. My
father didn't see his own sons birth he was to busy watching ball game on the
hospitles television. When I was three I was at a soft ball game and my brother
hit me with a baseball bat above my eye. The blood was spraying out like a
water foutain. When I got to the hospitle the doctors had to strap me up in a
stray jacket to keep me from hitting them. I ended up with about thirty stiches.
Sence I have two brothers and a sister I'm always busy, fighting them that is.
When I was five or six I was in the shower and I slipped on the soap SLAM! my
face smacked up against the side of the tub. I got stiched up with about 16 that
time. When somebody would ask me how I got the scare under my eye I don't

---

really want to tell them. Another thing that happened to me when I was about I'll say 7 I was playing wuffle ball and I was whating for my turn at bat so I sat on top of a low roof and fell off hurt my ankul the older kids payed no attention to me then finaly the ball game ended and they brought me home. When I got back they showed it to my mother and my foot was twice the size. So my mom brought me to the emergency room when I got there my sneaker wasn't on because It didn't fit me so everybody was staring at me like I was an alian. It took aboot an hour for the doctors to call me in. It ended out that I sprand my ankul I had to use crotches for 10 days at the most. Just resently I was shovleing the snow and I smashed in to a brick my shovel got stuck and I fell face first on the end of the shovel and now I have a big slash down my cheak. I'm suprised that I didn't get stiches. It sounds inposible but it happened pretty weird isn't it. I guese things go right some times I just can't think of any.

8. A Sonnet That Tells Me What I Want to Hear (Written during *The Newlywed Game*)

You are all that matters, the love that will end
all loves in my life forever and always. Forget children.
Forget my furry ex and his video game obsession.
Sit back and relax, honey, while I give you head.

It's true: I like a guy with no friends and books he
never reads. I'm into self-loathing and paranoid
jealousy. It's more important that we avoid
the world and spend all our time watching TV.

WELCOME BACK TO THE SHOW. WHEN IT COMES TO
YOUR MAN'S ELEVATOR SHAFT, WHAT BUILDING DOES IT
FIT BEST INSIDE? 1.) AN APARTMENT BUILDING,
I respect you. 2.) AN OFFICE COMPLEX, I love you.

Come to bed, baby. I need you. You're killing me.
Give me that big, hard 3.) EMPIRE STATE BUILDING.

9. My First Sonnet on Zoloft®

"NORMAL" she writes in quotes like it isn't measure-
able then draws a straight black line across the white board: ———
"All your life," she says, "or at least since fifteen years old—
you've been down around here, with feelings of displeasure,

panic, social anxiety disorder, depression,
thoughts of suicide, alcohol dependency,
and anhedonia. There have been, incidentally,
brief periods of time where you dropped even

lower to what's called a MAJOR DEPRESSIVE EPISODE,
bringing you somewhere more like down here: ———
for the span of several months or up to a year."
I nod politely. Twice now since devoting

myself to this, I've witnessed the limbs of a tree
smash the sun to a million glittering pieces.

10. Sonnet (Ending with My Grandmother's Pea Soup Recipe)

There's no rush. It's pretty simple. And it's
probably not gonna floor you, either—not the way
I was once when a slam poet slayed a crowd
of undergrads at a reading for extra credit

by spouting her mother's fried okra recipe
in six easy steps (with some flourishes about
love and justice). And why not? "There is no need
to explain or compare," William Carlos Williams wrote,

"Make it and it *is* a poem." Once she tried using Goya,
but after soaking the peas overnight she awoke
to little bugs "doing the backstroke," so she started going
to a feed store where people shop for their horses.

1 LB. YELLOW PEAS, WASHED THOROUGHLY AND SOAKED.
1 LARGE ONION (CHOPPED). WHITE RICE. SALT PORK OR CRISCO.

11. Sonnet (Written Before Her Parents Visit for the First Time)

Since they're going to sleep in our room, I ask Kay
if I should remove any books from the self-help shelf
beside the bed—ONE BREATH AT A TIME: BUDDHISM AND THE
    TWELVE
STEPS—I'm supposed to be anonymous anyway—

THE LANGUAGE OF LETTING GO: DAILY MEDI-
TATIONS FOR CODEPENDENTS—and it's not really
about me but other people's perceptions, and—
WHAT TO EXPECT WHEN YOU'RE EXPECTING—I've never read

them anyway; they're there with maybe twenty-five
other books I think I *should* read—I DON'T WANT TO TALK
ABOUT IT: OVERCOMING THE LEGACY OF MALE
DEPRESSION—but don't. Still, as a compromise

with myself, I flip the five suspects so all that's said
by THE BOOK OF QUITTING is on the blank fore edge.

12. Twelfth-Step Sonnet

When I asked the new guy at last night's meeting
how he was sleeping, he answered, "Not good. I was
overseas," like there's only one reason to leave
the US and only two places to go. "Iraq.

Two tours," he said. "There's no drinking, but there is
an all-you-can-eat Taco Bell. They treat us good."
I mistook his round face for someone younger.
He's a far cry from the wasp-waisted regimen Shaw

led to slaughter in what some around here call
the War of Northern Aggression. Most of the meeting
I thought of the "feelings aren't facts" maxim, wondering
how it applies to PTSD . . . *if* it does.

After the Lord's Prayer, I offered to be his sponsor.
"No, thanks. I'm only here because I have to be."

13. Sonnet (While Emptying Out
My Grandparents' House)

It wasn't the *Human Digest, Letters,* and *Response*
magazines in the rafters with cover stories
like "3-Way Marriage" and "Father Figure Sex Play"
nor the VHS-C tape in the bedroom drawer

labeled SEX VIDEO 4-29-00
that we found most surprising (in fact, that was expected),
    instead it was
in the spare room upstairs that my grandfather
drywalled himself in the first optimistic

days of Alzheimer's, where we found broken crack pipes
stashed along the inside molding of the closet
door and bottles of piss and cigarette butts
stuffed in the attic crawlspace, the blood red walls

stenciled in gold 平 神 爱 和 福
ending halfway across the wall on HAPPINESS.

14. Sonnet (with Language from My Daily Meditations)

Einstein probably never said most things people
are fond of attributing to him, especially
not his definition of insanity:
expecting a repeated action to equal

a different outcome. IT'S DISCOURAGING WHEN WE
ARE TRYING TO REMAKE OUR LIVES AND ALL WE CAN
SEE FOR OUR EFFORTS IS MINOR GROWTH. When I stand
up to share my frustration at a group meeting

I'm told by Ronnie the Vietnam vet to follow
in the bootprints of the person in front of me.
"Stay in the middle of the pack!" But still I think
of the other Einstein, who late in life went off alone

in search of a unifying theory and failed miser-
ably. I AM BECOMING THE MAN I ADMIRE.

15. Song from the Rooms

I tell John what I remember about my drinking
since devoting myself to this is its seclusion,
how I jammed a chair under the doorknob
as if to say, *You are all that matters, the love*

that will end all loves in my life forever.
Nobody fucking knew a thing. It's really about
other people's perceptions. What I think I was trying
to get at wasn't why we are so alone in our hurt,

cigarette butts stuffed in the attic crawlspace,
the blood red walls that we find most surprising,
instead it was expecting a repeated action
to equal a different outcome. It's pretty simple.

"There is no need to explain or compare," William
Carlos Williams wrote, "Make it and it *is* a prayer."

III ∘ A Treasury of Saints & Martyrs

Metamorphosis

1.

Grief arrives like a meeting I wonder how
I can get out of. This week four students died
in a 1 a.m. wreck heading back to campus
from the Cape. What's the lesson in it? I wonder.

How can I fit it to a narrative, place blame,
and explain it away when standing at the front
of a classroom full of freshmen who were their friends,
teammates, and maybe one, a first-week crush or mistake?

But there is no "teachable moment." Or the lesson
is too obvious and grim. The other driver
was going the wrong way. By the time they knew what
was coming at them—the white halogen lights

getting brighter in the rain—it was too late.
For two weeks, I mark everyone absent as *EA*.

2.

Emails go around with subject lines like HOW TO KNOW
IF YOU NEED EXTRA HELP WITH YOUR GRIEVING.
I say nothing to my students about it, and they
say nothing to me. Instead, I paraphrase the stories

they don't read. About the guy transformed into a bug,
a kid with a Southie accent comments, "That's weird."
The same thing he's said all semester about everything
we read. Things continue with an eerie normalcy

inside the class, while outside Campus Ministry
organizes a candlelight vigil on the Quad.
"What does it mean?" I ask. The news says the other driver
had her license suspended four times. But they retract

that story. After a pause, one student answers
hesitantly, "Maybe he brought it on himself somehow."

3.

Do you experience an ongoing sense of numbness?
an email asks anyone who will open it.
Do you feel isolated from yourself or others?
More articles fill in the details: A charred laptop

on the backseat, psychology notes on the floorboard.
One student wanted to be a firefighter
like the first responders who sawed open the crushed
Mercury Sable with the jaws of life in a nearby

salvage yard and extracted his body "with dignity."
We don't breathe a word about it in class.
Instead, they answer more questions about Gregor—
or "the bug-man," as he's come to be called.

"Maybe his family did it to him," one girl posits.
"They used him up and didn't care about his dreams."

4.

One of the students shared my name but spelled it *Kraig*.
There is a picture of him in the hall, smiling
with his family on Move-in Day. I look at it
and then I look to see who's looking at me.

Do your grief reactions continue, over time,
to be limited in some way? The other car
was an Infiniti G37. A scorched handbag
and melted cellphone on the passenger seat.

"But why?" I ask again. "Sometimes shit just happens,"
one student says. "The alarm goes off, but you don't
wake up. Or, you wake up as a bug or whatever."
For the first time, Southie offers something different:

"Maybe it's not about *why*. Maybe it's about
how everybody left behind just has to deal with it."

Fishbone Novena

—for Saint Blaise, patron saint of animals
and those suffering from throat ailments

1.

Come, O Saint Stammerer, Saint Stutterer,
Patron Saint of the Lisp and Smokeswept Throat,
Patron Saint of the Zookeeper and Marine Biologist,
Patron Saint of No-Known-Relation—

Pray for Florida Pest Control and the Department
of Environmental Protection; pray for the Fish,
Game, and Wildlife Commission; pray for the animal
control officer who grips the snare pole he slips

like a whisper around the neck of a raccoon,
possum, red fox, river otter, armadillo,
alligator, muskrat, fisher cat, or coyote
with its hidden litter of pups under the porch steps.

He tightens the snare around the neck of each and drags
them one by one across the field of stones to safety.

2.

One day a group of hunters seeking wild
animals for the amphitheater came upon
Blaise's cave in the woods. They were surprised
then frightened to see the bishop kneeling in prayer

surrounded by lions and bears. Lame animals
made their way to him in herds to be healed.

As the hunters dragged him off to prison, they came
across a suckling pig squealing for its life

in the jaws of a wolf. At Blaise's command,
the beast released the baby and it returned,
miraculously restored, to its owner,
a poor, frail woman who later thanked Blaise

by bringing two wax candles to dispel the gloom
of the cell where he waited to be executed.

3.

Once a month, a graduate student rescues me
from my sixth-grade science class where we are studying
endangered species. She takes me to the coat closet
to correct my "slushy esses" by levering

a wooden depressor against my bottom teeth
and forcing my tongue to the roof of my mouth.
"I see seven Saimaa ringed seals swimming swiftly." *Good.*
"I see six scientists studying seasonal snowfall." *Good.*

"I see some sea otters straining to say something:
'These six-pack soda rings are strangling me!'" *Good.*
"I see a single dusky seaside sparrow singing:
'Mosquito insecticides surround the space center.'" *Good.*

"I see a Polynesian tree snail slowly slide down
the inside of its plastic box, last of its species." *Good. Good.*

4.

Another story coming from the medical journal
of Aëtius Amidenus references
Saint Blaise as a doctor who gave up his practice·
to serve as bishop of Armenia.

In this one, Blaise wasn't accidently discovered
in his cave but hunted down by henchmen
of the Roman emperor Licinius,
who wanted to make an example of his piety.

Blaise was being marched to the capital in chains
when he and the bounty hunters came across
a mother whose son was doubled over in the road,
a fishbone stuck in his throat. Panicked,

she pushed through the guards and threw herself at the feet
of the future martyr: "Please help us . . . Oh, please . . ."

5.

Come, O Saint Slurrer, Saint Something-or-other.
From the desire to be invisible,

from the fear of being forgotten,
from the fear of being invisible,

from the desire to be forgotten,
from the fear of controls and the desire to control,
deliver us, Saint Blaise.
So that others may be more invisible.

So that others may be better forgotten.
So that the pups shall remain forever beneath the steps (or for
    as long as they desire).
So that that boy won't be forced to stay forever in the closet—
    his tongue banished to the alveolar ridge
repeating calamities to empty coats smelling of last night's dinner.

Grant us, Saint Blaise, the capacity
for joy, empathy, and mercy.

6.

When I get home from school, instead of studying
for his GED, my uncle is on the top porch
showing my brothers how to break the bottom off
a Michelob bottle and jab some motherfucker

in the face should a gang, for instance, roll up
when you're walking home alone from a friend's house.
"A lot of people think you take out the big one
first, but that's bullshit. It's the loud one

you have to worry about. He's the leader.
Take him down and the rest will follow. Like this,"
he says, firmly tapping the base of the brown bottle
against a concrete planter full of dead flowers.

Fragments of glass rain down on the front gate
some piece of shit is always leaving open.

7.

O Patron Saint of Wildlife Management,
O Patron Saint of Hook, Line, and Sinker,
O Patron Saint of Panda Bear Husbandry,
O Patron Saint of 1-800-PET-MEDS,

Saint Blaise, tell us the words that you said
when the mother came to you and pled, "Oh, please . . ."
When the loudest hunter said, "Enough! Come with me . . ."
When you first said the words to dislodge the bone

lodged like an unpronounceable word in the young
boy's throat. Tell us what grabbed hold

of that tiny bough, slowly pulled it back like a bow,
and let go. What prayer fell like two white candles

across the kid's sorry esophagus as he coughed:
Ahem! Hack! Hack! Hack! Hack! Umphgg!

8.

Like Jesus, Blaise walked on water, but unlike Jesus,
when he got to the center of the lake, he sat down.
Saint Blaise had more style. From the iron comb dragged
across his flesh, thin strips fell from his shoulders

and back like wood shavings strewn about the square
that the faithful secretly swiped up and saved
as souvenirs. Asked a last time what spell he cast
to save the boy, Blaise sat silent on the scaffold,

though the mother stepped forward on the saint's behalf:
"He simply said, 'God loves you.'" The executioner
was signaled then to drive his weighted axe blade down.
It took seven tries to sever head from body.

During this time, Blaise blessed the flies buzzing in his ears
and invited them to lay their eggs in his neck.

9.

There's no mention of what happened to the animals
after Blaise's death. They must have gotten tired
of waiting for his return and slowly dispersed.
Like most things, they did fine once left alone.

The crocodile found the plover bird to remove
the decaying meat from its teeth. The zebra
got the oxpecker to pick ticks from its rough hide.
The human race continued as before, descaling

and choking on the splintered skeletons of fish
dragged up indiscriminately by trawler nets
and spilled onto ship decks. Their panicky eyes
would have to wait two millennia for the world

to return their stare. Then twelve billion would gasp,
searching for a single breath in a world of air.

What It Was Like, What Happened, and What It's Like Now

1.

You sit on a three-legged stool at the front
of the room—three-time cancer survivor, double
mastectomy, fifteen years married, twenty sober—
hair so thin from the treatments the light shines

through it, giving the appearance of an aura
to symbolize your suffering, I think. I think
your hair used to be darker. Your aura too . . .
if those things change. You probably loved the sun

because you remind me of my friend's older sister
who took us as kids on daytrips to the beach.
"I can't have kids," you say without skipping a beat,
like you've said it a thousand times before.

1:30 P.M.: HE SPEAKS TO HIS ASSISTANT ON THE PHONE.
SHE REPORTS EVERYTHING "SEEMED FINE."

2.

The news is all about the latest actor to die
with a needle in his arm. Rumor has it they found
fifty bags of heroin from New York or New Jersey
with skulls on them—provisions for the week ahead.

In Worcester, it's one or two bags at a time—
one con, petty theft, or misdemeanor sex act

at a time—and still eight dead last week alone.
Almost nine if what the kid next to me says is true.

He was in a bed at UMass Medical
all week with a blood infection. I want to learn
to trust people, but he acts like every addict
I've ever known who wants something.

2:00 P.M.: MOTHER OF HIS THREE CHILDREN SEES HIM
OUTSIDE HIS APARTMENT. REPORTS HE "SEEMED HIGH."

3.

You tell us about your teen years rummaging through
suburban houses for whatever you could find.
What happened was you got sent to Syracuse.
Four times to Syracuse. You've been through the ringer,

you say, and you're finally finished deferring
to others for what you know enough about.
On the way to the beach, I'd studied my friend's sister
from the backseat of their mother's Chevette

until she became my first crush. For two hours
in the sun and breeze, her tanned left leg extended
out the window, Achilles' heel nestled snug
between the driver's side mirror and the door.

5:00 P.M.: SPOTTED IN STREET BY AN ACQUAINTANCE.
THEY SAY "HI" AND EXCHANGE AN AWKWARD HIGH FIVE.

4.

"Understanding is a booby prize," you say.
I silently agree. All the kid who nearly died
learned by nearly dying is that he nearly died.
Done with chemo since July, you say you have just

started to feel okay saying "fuck it" again.
9:00 P.M.: IN SIX TRANSACTIONS, HE WITHDRAWS $1,200
FROM A SUPERMARKET ATM. At first, I imagined
what the wind felt like on her feet. Then I imagined

I was the wind. You straighten up on your stool
and smile: "Saying 'fuck it' can be a spiritual act."
"Fuck it," the kid next to me says under his breath
and leaves without getting anyone to sign his sheet.

9:00 A.M.: FAILS TO PICK UP HIS CHILDREN FROM
THEIR MOTHER'S HOUSE. HIS NO-SHOW CAUSES CONCERN.

A Short History of Artists in My Family

1.

We've only had one really. My mom's cousin Ronnie
who I almost never saw growing up. I was told
he went away to college in Boston and came back
bloated with a sick liver from the drinking.

A cautionary tale about artistic ambitions,
college, cities, and addiction. In the early '90s
we learned he was in the same room as his sister
when she OD'd on heroin. The lack of any

further details made it worse than if we had known
every juicy bit. He was in and out of shelters
after that. My brother would spot him downtown
while pouring concrete. "Guess who I saw hobbling

up the street on one crutch today?" he'd ask,
setting up the punchline with a smirk. "The artist!"

2.

I never had a clue about what kind of art
he made other than the two landscape paintings
he gave my grandparents during a brief stint when he'd
"gotten his shit together." My grandfather built frames

for them in the cellar, meticulously smoothing
the edges of the wood with fine-grade sandpaper,
applying three coats of a dark walnut stain,
then going over that with a polyurethane

that stunk up the stairwell for a week. He hung them
side by side above a couch with its own woodland
scene I used to get lost in. Stepping back to make
sure they were level, he gave me the closest thing

I ever got to an art education: "That's not
really how leaves look," he said, "but it's still nice."

3.

Ronnie was dead for a year before anyone in
our clan knew. "Couldn't someone have reached out?
It's not like we are a small group," his niece asked.
The obit sent around mistakenly said he

was born in Canada on August 20, 1049.
There was mention of a PCA and caregiver,
and no one else. "He was very private," his brother
added as an explanation. "They probably

just didn't know who to contact." Someone posted
a link to a video set to music. The cellphone
hovered over a bedroom wall covered with ink
drawings on postcards set meticulously apart—

they had the tortured intricacy of prison art,
abstract as the idea of hunger to one who starves.

The World's Longest Poem (*Abridged*)

1.

There once was a boy who wanted to write
the world's longest poem. To do that, he knew
he would have to throw everything he had into it.
He started to diagram the flock patterns

of the birds that passed overhead—robins, starlings,
and geese—then he mapped the white clover flowers
that sprung up among the shiny cleats of every
soccer field his sisters chased a checkered ball across,

balancing the blossom carefully upon each
like the dot that floats over the stem of a lowercase i.
All kinds of characters made cameos in the poem
whose jagged right edge came to mirror the notches

of a key that he could use to unlock the door
of whatever hospital room he was stuck inside.

2.

The first prompt in *Opening Up by Writing It Down:
How Expressive Writing Improves Health and Eases
Emotional Pain* asks the reader to write about
"a stressful or upsetting experience in life."

I think of the "help me" moment. Although I already
talked through it with my brother at IHOP
the morning after, the more I think about it
the more uncertain I become. What if Alex

wasn't simply asking me to scooch him up
in bed, as Luke assured me. What if he was asking
for help of another kind? Maybe he thought that
I, his wise old uncle, held some secret trick

to end his suffering. Maybe he was asking
for something he thought only I could give.

3.

On my way to the hospital, I am speaking
a text message into my phone when I get pulled
over by a statie. My cat stretches out bored
on the heated passenger seat as I roll down

the window and she meows at his stupid hat.
"Sorry," I say looking at Ms. E. He asks if I saw him
back there, and I say yes even though I didn't.
"If you saw me, how come you didn't slow down?"

Sometimes the truth sounds like a lie, but I say it
anyway and hate myself for it: "I'm heading to see

my nephew who's sick. I guess I was distracted."
Back in his dark SUV, he writes my ticket.

"You were going too fast to ignore," he says,
then adds: "Fight it if you want. I won't be there."

4.

On the eighth floor of Connecticut Children's
Medical Center, a girl in the arts and crafts room
is making slime with the rest of the kids. Her iPad
is propped up in front of her so she can watch

a comedy just released on Netflix.
She is talking more with the art therapist
than with the children; if it wasn't for her wristband,
I'd mistake her for a volunteer or employee.

"I should turn this off," she says, wiping her fingers.
"Isn't he in *Modern Family*?" the therapist asks.
"Yeah . . ." she says, then adds that she turned twenty this week
and no one in her family came to visit.

"They're busy. I get it," she says, reflexively
mixing glue, water, and green food coloring again.

5.

Eddie Shore III is in Alex's room when I get there.
He is heir to another man's achievements,
meaning his grandfather was a hockey great.
He and the teenager with him are in sweatpants.

Each has a candy bar to tear open as
they launch into a familiar shtick: "Colton and I
were having a debate on our drive here today.
I was saying Hershey's is the best chocolate bar.

Colton thinks it's Mars." They take exaggerated
bites while throwing out descriptors like *rich* and *creamy*.
"Here, chief, will you help settle this once and for all?"
Eddie III extends the partially eaten candy

to the wary boy looking at him like a con man
trying to lure him into a game he doesn't want to play.

6.

I bring Alex the most expensive pen and pad
I could find at the crafts store. When he visited
my house a few years ago and saw the shelves
of books and the messy desk, he fell in love with

the writer's life and instantly started dreaming
of a scenario where he would move in and we

would do nothing but work on our books all day.
I didn't have the heart to tell him I was the kind

of writer no one reads, and as he and Luke drove
the darkening backroads home, I let myself get lost
in a child's fleeting fantasy that we would one day
team up to write the world's longest poem—

passing it back and forth over years and years
until it outgrew either of our wildest dreams.

7.

My aunt is annoying everyone with talk of
the Budwig Diet again. She wants to liquefy flaxseed
and cottage cheese and pour it down Alex's tube.
"She was nominated for the Nobel Prize

seven times," she says, "but big pharma doesn't want
a cure. There's too much money to be made." I can't
believe she has me sympathizing with Pfizer,
but her "research" methods leave much to be desired.

She says she'll send Luke a link to a YouTube video
that basically proves that when following protocol
there's a 90 percent success rate. My own research
links Johanna Budwig's Wikipedia page

to the one for Quack, from the Dutch *kwak*, an idiom
going back to the Middle Ages, meaning "to shout."

8.

When Alex said "help me" it was a whisper
through a little boy's cracked lips. Yes, it's likely
he was just asking for a boost. It's possible, too,
he was asking for something else—his mom and dad

momentarily out of the room. He had been
holding on for twenty-nine months. He was tired
like few ever know. Could I help him to let go
of what he had only ever known to hold on to?

"Write for 20 or 30 minutes, focusing
on your deepest emotions and thoughts about
a stressful or upsetting experience in your life."
At the center of the whirlpool is a shaft of air.

I listen to the echoing swoosh of sound,
trying to decipher the faint voice inside.

9.

This husband and wife are the last people
you would expect to be making a drug deal

in the parking lot of the farmers' market on
a Thursday evening. But there they are in the black

minivan, buying gelcaps half filled with resin
prepared by an equally inconspicuous soccer mom.
"I couldn't ask anyone to give their children
what they aren't willing to try themselves," she says.

"Besides, I need to know you're not undercover."
She laughs as they wash down a capsule each with some
Dr. Pepper, and they browse the tables while it kicks in.
"Cool, huh?" a farmer says. "It's called Buddha's hand."

The man picks up the ugly lemon that looks like the tumor
tightening its fifteen fingers around his son's brain.

10.

Luke texts me in the middle of the afternoon:
"Heard from Bobby Orr today. He's stopping over
to visit Alex tomorrow at 11am."
Celebrity athletes have a sixth sense, I think.

The greater they are, the closer we are to the end.
I don't say this to my brother, of course. Instead:
"That's so cool . . . I'll be working in the yard ☺ "
Bobby Orr is my nephew's favorite hockey player

even though he's too young to have seen him play.
It's all about that one image. When Orr visits
he brings a stack of glossies to sign for every
classmate. A give-and-go pass, a Stanley Cup–winning

goal, and a skinny kid in skates flies through the air,
transformed forever into a superhero.

11.

MEGATRON, SPONGEBOB, AND MICHELANGELO
WERE IN FIRST GRADE TOGETHER. MICHELANGELO
SAID, "LET'S GO TO THE PIZZA SHOP." MEGATRON
SAID, "I'LL DRIVE!" AND SPONGEBOB SAID, "I'LL SWIM!"

WHEN THEY GOT THERE, THEY HAD A HARD TIME DECIDING
WHAT TOPPINGS TO GET. SPONGEBOB WANTED KRABBY PATTIES,
MICHELANGELO WANTED A DELUXE PIZZA,
AND MEGATRON WANTED PEPPERONI AND CHEESE.

THEY BEGAN TO ARGUE OVER WHICH PIZZA WAS BEST.
SPONGEBOB PUT MEGATRON IN A HEADLOCK.
THE PEOPLE EATING IN THE PIZZA SHOP WERE SHOCKED.
FINALLY, MICHELANGELO REALIZED, "WE COULD

EACH GET OUR OWN PIZZA WITH WHATEVER WE WANT ON IT."
"THIS IS WHY WE'RE BEST FRIENDS!" THEY ALL SAID TOGETHER.

12.

Thirty years after Saint Anthony's death he was
dug up, and even though his body had turned to dust,
his tongue was still moist and glistening. Eight hundred
years later, my aunt claims to have a piece of it.

She won't tell anyone how she got it. Anthony
of Padua lived in a hut under a walnut tree
and died at the age of thirty-five from eating
infected barley that turned to fire in his gut.

"It's a first-class relic," my aunt says. But, it's not
the thing we are to worship, warns the Catholic Church:
"We venerate the relics of the martyrs in order
to better adore Him whose martyrs they are."

I'd pay to see a bureaucrat from the Vatican
come to my aunt's cul-de-sac to tell her that.

13.

Alex is still with us a few weeks later
when I see the trooper's face flash on the TV.
The local news reports his Explorer was struck
on the highway as he "processed a motor vehicle stop."

After a few days of half-mast flags and weeks
of public reverence and mourning, his widow starts

to appear in TV ads urging "Vote NO on 4."
In front of a fireplace of unlit ceramic logs,

she plays up her working-class Boston accent:
"With this bill there's going to be more fatalities.
There's going to be more of us without our
loved ones. If it can happen to my family,

it can happen to anyone. Why risk it now?
Vote NO to Marijuana in Massachusetts."

14.

Last week a video of Tom Brady in Monaco
went viral. He was dressed in skin-tight white jeans
and a Eurotrash mesh half-shirt, throwing
a football fifty yards from one yacht to another.

This week the GOAT has recorded a video
just for our boy. Now he dons the washed-out
earth-tone polo shirt of New England and stands
in front of a brick wall with a touch of ivy.

"Hey Alex! What's up, man? I hear you're the biggest
Patriots fan out there and you like the Bruins, too.
And I just want to let you know I'm a fan of you.
And I just love you, I support you, we've got your back.

We're going to win a bunch of games for you this year."
His all-American smile flashes white as death.

15.

There once was a boy who wanted to write
the world's longest poem. To do that, he knew
he would have to ignore the boundaries imposed
by form, tradition, and the publishing world.

Some words he stretched taut as powerlines,
while others he harnessed to worms to be dragged
to the purple sadness at the center of the earth.
Characters appeared out of nowhere to add

some excitement whenever things got stale.
Megatron, SpongeBob, and Michelangelo would
swoop in on a spaceship using the poem's words as fuel,
gurgling them up and spewing out a vapor trail:

G B Y S W P D I L Y M
A H O P B A Y I J N A

F

G

F   Y   I   M

X   A   J   D

J

L

Q

V   Y

P   K

67

K

H

X

G

Z

T

M

V

U

So long, A. B.

IV ∘ Silver Millennium

Magnolia Room

1.

The flower on the bedside table lights up the book
Kay flips through back to front, lost in the image
of a girl with a pet crow sweeping dead leaves
around the shrine where she lives with her grandfather.

The petals open like white pages coming loose
from the hardened glue of the binding. I can't look
and I can't turn away from the constant glow
over her shoulder like a ghost in the distance.

Her rapt attention is equal parts memory
and escape. Part real, part fantasy. Part trauma,
part recovery. I want a voice as plain and free
from judgment as the vending machine in the lobby

when it drops our key with a rattle and says:
Welcome to Magnolia Room. Please enjoy your stay.

2.

Like countless English teachers before me
I tell my students that *stanza* in Italian
means *room*, suggesting to them that I know Italian
and that words are like furniture or flowers

that the lonely poet painstakingly arranges
to entice the reader inside, to sit down

in the corner chair with a cold drink
and forget everything else designed to distract.

When this doesn't work, I tell the class that *stanza*
in Italian means *crime scene*. All we know for sure
is something happened, so slip some plastic bags
on your feet and let the evidence speak to you.

A partial shoeprint on the petal on the floor
might be nothing, or it might break the case wide open.

3.

When I point out the magnolia tree in bloom
on the hill, Kay says it reminds her of the scene
in the public garden from her favorite anime.
The male lead runs into his childhood friend—

whose name in Italian means *flower*—and his girlfriend
gets jealous because, in all their years together,
he never mentioned him even once. I think
of everything we don't share until, one day, we do.

Memory is like the blue baseball hat on the kid
sitting on his father's shoulders as he climbs uphill
for a photo in front of the tree. He takes one picture
with it on and one with it off. Then it slips

from his fingers into the grass, as the white flowers,
too, like a thousand bows, all untie and fall free.

4.

Poems are for the dead, I tell my class. Like flowers,
they grow on trees, surprise us sometimes with strange
beauty, but mostly go unnoticed before floating
to the ground to get mowed up with grass clippings

and sent to the dump. Once gone, it's as if a poem,
like a single flower, never even existed—
just as every person is eventually forgotten.
This explains the poem-flower-death connection.

For those so far untouched by mortality, I share
a quote by Simone Weil: "Never to think of a being
we love, but have not actually before our eyes,
without reflecting that perhaps this person is dead."

A student in the backrow texts her girlfriend,
the pulsing • • • telling her all she needs to know.

5.

After losing touch, the friend searched the galaxy
for a flower worthy of their childhood love.
He ended up on a comet where he became possessed
by a parasitic plant that leeches on to its host

and forces it to do its bidding. In this way,
evil spreads throughout the universe one planet
at a time, appearing no different from the beauty
it destroys. The story could end on this hard fact

if not for the show's requisite final transformations
and battle scenes that close each episode
and drive home the lie that good always beats evil.
Cue the blue-haired villain sprung forth from a pistil

to shoot vines that twist around the limbs of the teens
writhing into the final commercial break.

6.

It's okay to get bored by a poem, a flower,
or a person—especially if that person is yourself,
or a version of yourself you can't stand to look
at anymore. I tell my students to turn the page

if they don't like a poem. Swipe left. I confess
to them that I don't read most of the poems
on the Academy of American Poets page.
Who has the time? There's no need to click every link

or dog-ear every page. Besides, some poems,
like this one, go on for too long, always adding

one more counterfeit jewel to an already
overwrought crown. The words on the other side

of the page are visible as ghosts . . . as invisible
as ghosts . . . calling us, either way, to their world.

7.

When Kay excitedly puts in the VHS cassette
she got in the mail from her mother, suddenly
an elementary school version of her is sitting
straight-backed at a desk delivering the "Moon News."

I can't bear to watch her home movies any more
than I can watch my own. How she throws her head back
in laughter is too unrecoverable to consider.
As is the knowledge of what her smile hides.

Her newscast, like the real news, is a litany of deaths
and how they happened. She tells the camera that,
after breaking free, the troop of teen heroes flew
in a bubble to a comet to kill the parasite.

Once restored, the long-lost friend opened his hand
and from his palm a beautiful white flower bloomed.

8.

The flower on the bedside table falls open
like it could give a fuck . . . like it couldn't give a fuck.
It relaxes open openly like flowers do,
which are unlike ghosts, with their constant

appeals to be noticed, to be something they're not—
friendly, solid, observable bodies—instead
of being what they really are: barely there.
Petals drop like life rafts from the side of a ship.

Kay picks one up and uses it as a bookmark
in the manga she hasn't stopped reading since
third grade, and on our way out of the room
she steps on a second petal by the door.

The flower on the bedside table falls open
like it holds no special power whatsoever.

Moon News

1.

My own home movies preserve three instances of grown
men pulling their pants down and showing their asses
to the camera. I know this because I recently
rewatched eight hours to make a video

as a wedding gift for my sister. In the end
Kay and I decided to include only one mooning:
my uncle standing on the shore of a river
as the camera cuts to my infant sister in a bonnet

sitting on a blanket with a disembodied arm
holding a bottle to her mouth. The 35mm
cuts back to my uncle, then my sister again, until finally
he smiles, thumbs the fly of his jeans, and turns around.

Today, Jeff Bezos said we are returning to the moon.
It's our only hope, he says, to save humanity.

2.

The history of the moon didn't begin with men
landing on it. But you wouldn't know that
by listening to the news. This week it's all about
Apollo 11. Last week it was moon stones

stowed in city hall filing cabinets and forgotten
about, or snuck home like priceless works of stolen art

and hidden so well they became lost to everyone.
Oh well, the moon was never Richard Nixon's

to give away like bags of sand from a beach
he didn't visit to begin with. Just so you know:
the moon appeared after earth took a glancing blow
off the chin 4.5 billion years ago.

Every day since it has been tugging at our seas
like a child afraid its mother will leave.

The Silver Age

after Hesiod

It was a time when humans played like children
upon the earth, safeguarded for a hundred years
by helicopter parents who latched the oven doors
and plugged the electrical outlets with red clay.

When they finally arrived at their long-delayed
adolescence, they could no longer be protected
from themselves; they lived recklessly and refused
to obey the laws of the gods and of nature. Zeus,

looking down from Mount Olympus, had had enough:
"I'd rather watch an ash tree grow for a thousand years
than see these fools on parade for one more day."
This race dwells in the ground now, their legacy

weathered by those who came after with the adage:
They did the best they could with what they had.

NOTES

The quote from *Saturday Night Live* in section 5 of "I Hate Myself and Want to Die" is from a "Deep Thoughts by Jack Handey" segment first broadcast on November 10, 1990.

The quoted lines in the third stanza of "Sonnet (with Language Etched into the Corner of a Bus Window)" are from Walt Whitman's "Song of Myself," section 6.

The William Carlos Williams lines quoted in "Birthday Night Sonnet" and "Sonnet (Ending with My Grandmother's Pea Soup Recipe)" and adapted in "Song from the Rooms" are from *The Descent of Winter*, "11/1: Introduction": "That thing, the vividness which is poetry by itself, makes the poem. There is no need to explain or compare. Make it and it *is* a poem. This is modern, not the saga. There are no sagas—only trees now, animals, engines: There's that."

"Oh Lovely Rock (a Sonnet with a Phone Number in It)" takes the first part of its title from the Robinson Jeffers poem of the same name.

"Sonnet (While Emptying Out My Grandparents' House)" ends with five Chinese characters that translate roughly to: 平 (peace), 神 (god), 爱 (love), 和 (harmony), and 福 (happiness).

"Sonnet (with Language from My Daily Meditations)" has language from the March 8 entry of *Touchstones: A Book of Daily Meditations for Men* (Hazelden Publishing).

The timeline used in "What It Was Like, What Happened, and What It's Like Now" was drawn, with minor editing, from CNN's article "Piecing Together Philip Seymour Hoffman's Final Hours" (February 4, 2014).

Section 11 of "The World's Longest Poem *(Abridged)*" was written by Alexander Blais (2006–2018).

Quoted language in section 12 of "The World's Longest Poem *(Abridged)*" is attributed to Saint Jerome. The book *Opening Up by Writing It Down: How Expressive Writing Improves Health and Eases Emotional Pain* referred to in the poem was written by James W. Pennebaker, PhD, and Joshua M. Smyth, PhD.

"The Silver Age" is a loose translation of lines from Hesiod's "The Five Ages," in *Works and Days*.